A Prayer for Forgiving My Parents

A Prayer for Forgiving My Parents

Poems by

Daun Daemon

© 2023 Daun Daemon. All rights reserved.
This material may not be reproduced in any form, published,
reprinted, recorded, performed, broadcast,
rewritten or redistributed without
the explicit permission of Daun Daemon.
All such actions are strictly prohibited by law.

Cover design by Shay Culligan
Cover image by George Bonev
Author photo by Al Sutton

ISBN: 978-1-63980-357-6

Kelsay Books
502 South 1040 East, A-119
American Fork, Utah 84003
Kelsaybooks.com

In memory of John Foster West—poet, novelist, short story writer, folklorist, teacher, mountain man, yellow dog, and my beloved great-uncle who always encouraged me but didn't live forever, as I thought he would, to see me become a published poet.

This is for you, Uncle John, as you eternally cruise the Blue Ridge Parkway in your MG roadster with the top down, Scottish tartan scarf floating in the wind, tweed newsboy cap snug on your bald head, handlebar mustache twitching as you curse at the autumn leaf peepers and Florida license plates.

Acknowledgments

Thank you to my friends and colleagues for support and encouragement—Rod, Kathleen, Barb, Catherine, Mel, Elizabeth, the knitters, and so many more; to Peggy, my twinning friend and poet sister, for guiding me; to Patrice, my soul sister, for putting down your book and talking to me; and to Russ, my navigator, for holding my hand.

To D & D, these poems tell my story—you have your own stories to tell.

PUBLICATIONS

I offer endless appreciation to the editors who have published my poems:

45 Magazine Women's Literary Journal: "Well-Bred"

Black Poppy Review: "After I slept in Mama and Daddy's bed," "Reiki"

CP Quarterly: "All Kinds of Crazy Critters," "Eat up with it"

The Dead Mule School of Southern Literature: "Duchess, a German Shepherd Dog," "Through the Mill Village, 1973"

Deep South Magazine: "Double-Jointed," "On Trying to Write a Prayer for Forgiving My Parents," "That First Poem"

Dime Show Review: "Between the Sheets"

Harpy Hybrid Review: "This is why I'm telling you about the wiener dog"

Memoryhouse Magazine: "Too Many Kittens"

Origami Poems: "I hear her voice calling"

Peeking Cat: "Bats," "When Mama Sang 'Mockingbird Hill'"

Perspectives Magazine: "The Beauty Shop Money Box"

The Poet: "Different Daddies"

Remington Review: "A Prayer for a Good Day in the Beauty Shop, 1975," "Kaleidoscope," "Please don't cut down the cedar tree," "To the elderly hairdresser"

Synaeresis Arts + Poetry: "In the Beauty Shop, 1963–2006"

Third Wednesday Magazine: "Hens"

Typehouse: "Dead Air," "I called you bastard for eight reasons," "Pixie"

Typishly: "My Daddy Taught Me to Pack"

Willawaw Journal: "By flowers"

AWARDS & RECOGNITION

"I hear her voice calling" was awarded 1st place in the 2017 Origami Poems Project Kindness Contest.

"My Daddy Taught Me to Pack" received a Pushcart Prize nomination in 2018.

Contents

THE SESSION

Reiki   17

BEFORE THE BOTTLE

At Three   21
When Mama Sang "Mockingbird Hill"   23
Between the Sheets   24
Pet of the Week   25
Double-Jointed   26
Bats   27

REFUGE

[untitled haiku]   31
A Prayer for a Good Day in the Beauty Shop, 1975   32
In the Beauty Shop, 1963–2006   33
All Kinds of Crazy Critters   34
Eat up with it   35
Hens   36
Pixie   37
Duchess, a German Shepherd Dog   39
The Beauty Shop Money Box   40
Dead Air   41

DADDY

My Daddy Taught Me to Pack   45
Too Many Kittens   47
In Deepest Sympathy   48
Different Daddies   49
Daddy's Little Girl   50

Weeping Forsythia — 51
[Noise] — 52
I called you "bastard" for eight reasons — 53
This is why I'm telling you about the wiener dog — 55

MAMA, AFTER DADDY

To the elderly hairdresser — 63
Obituary: Mickey's Beauty Salon, Hudson, NC, 1963–2012 — 65
After I slept in Mama and Daddy's bed — 67
I hear her voice calling — 68
Please don't cut down the cedar tree — 70
Wash her hair — 72
By flowers — 73
Mama's Baby — 74

LEGACY

Armored — 77
Well-Bred — 78
My Feral Children — 79
That First Poem — 80
My Mama Taught Me to Smile — 81
Every Other Sunday at 4 — 83

THE PRAYER

On Trying to Write a Prayer for Forgiving My Parents — 87

"Children begin by loving their parents.
After they grow older, they judge them;
sometimes they forgive them."

—Oscar Wilde, *The Picture of Dorian Gray*

THE SESSION

Reiki

he touched my head with searching hands
heat pulsing like an aura across skin
he entered me—a seeker, a healer, a medium
      pushing through skin, journeying into blood and memory
      my brain a tangled story of father, mother, then, now,
      loss and ache embedded in tissues, cells, synapses
      in those spaces inside, in the dark, dark darkness
      I felt him reaching, finding, seeing, knowing
afterwards, he said I burned his hands,
offered a prayer for forgiving parents,
but his prayer was all about me

BEFORE THE BOTTLE

At Three

before the beauty shop was built

When I was three, I pedaled my tricycle
around the patio beneath the old pear tree,
its plump flower buds beginning to open.

You glanced at me from where you ironed
all the way at the other end of the house,
through the long living room, in the kitchen.

Daddy was at work, my sisters at school.
I was alone with you—except for the kittens
tumbling nearby—you were mine alone.

Whenever I turned to look, you were there,
smiling, assuring me that I was safe so far
away from you, outside while you were in.

I turned five tight circles on the concrete,
because I could count that high, and watched
my Mary Janes go round and round.

When the last circle was turned, I looked
to see if you were proud of me, your big girl
who could ride her tricycle on the patio.

You weren't there.

On the ironing board, the iron stood upright,
its plug dangling above the floor.

You weren't there.

I was alone for the first time.
For the first time, I was all alone.

I waited for you and waited for you
and then, feet on the pedals, I pushed.

When Mama Sang "Mockingbird Hill"

Mama festooned the house
with her singing, draping her trills
and warbles over the furniture
like strands of sun-kissed roses
strewn over a dew-covered hill

She filled my heart with happiness
because *she* was happy when she sang,
all the world peaceful and still,
brimming with the goodness
of her thrilling mockingbird lilt

Now I wake to birds in the springtime
in the trees near my windowsill—
though their songs aren't as lovely
as the tra-la-la and tweedlee dee dee
of my mother singing her song to me

Between the Sheets

When Mama washed the sheets, she stripped beds bare,
toted a basket brimming with linens to the back yard. On
those summer mornings in the Carolina foothills, I watched
from our pecan tree's shade, grasshoppers flying and fiddling
in air thick as biscuit gravy, as Mama pinned the sheets
to four steel cables strung between two concrete t-posts.

My sisters stayed inside, painting their toenails peony pink
or forget-me-not blue, flipping through magazines revealing
how to pad bras and flirt with boys, whispering secrets. When I,
too young for the bedroom talk of teenaged girls, skulked
outside the window, they hushed, cranked up their radio's
volume, and screamed the raucous tunes of British boy bands.

Later as Mama tried to fetch the sheets, I raced between them,
flapping the fabric with my elbows. Mama pretended to lose
sight of me, searched up and down the rows of cotton flowers
and stripes, singing *where is she? where is she hiding?*
all the while knowing her baby girl was there between the sheets
because I giggled and could not quiet my flip-flopping feet.

As daylight faded and lightning bugs rose like steam outside
my open bedroom window, I folded myself into the scent of love
and sunshine, waited for Mama to tuck me in. *Sleep tight, don't
let the bed bugs bite* she said every night, her voice a lullaby's
melody. I giggled, kicked my feet in the sheets as she pulled
the door and left it ajar, a line of light pushing through the dark.

Pet of the Week

for Virginia B., she who inspired my eternal cat love

These fifty-plus years later,
I read the newspaper clipping's headline,
wonder if readers thought *I* was
"Pet of the Week!"—
the black & white photo featuring
a beaming 8-year-old me
sitting on the hardwood floor,
legs daintily tucked to the side,
pretty plaid dress carefully hiding all
but the tips of my Oxfords,
with a tabby cat displayed on a blanket,
five assorted kittens nursing furiously at her belly,
her head turned away from the camera
in that instant of intimate mothering

Ribbon tied around my pageboy,
bangs skimming my brows,
I looked the proud mama myself,
waiting for the day I nurtured my own young,
photographs capturing lives
destined to yellow in musty photo albums
through decades of darkness—
but I remained childless,
becoming mother of feral cats and kittens,
brushing fur instead of braiding hair,
pouring kibble instead of cereal into bowls,
outliving all but the few that lounge
on the sun porch or curl into my husband's lap
and nap like babies

Double-Jointed

I was an origami child,
folding myself into shapes:
wedging elbows behind ears,
tucking knees behind elbows,
balancing on butt bones
like a docked-tail crane.

Mama commanded performances
for elderly visitors and relatives
like Aunt Edna, a fleshy woman
who found my folds and pleats
as charming as the layered frills
on her fancy Sunday frock.

"She's double-jointed!" Mama said,
as if it were an accomplishment
and not a trick of hypermobility
played on overly proud parents
eager for their children to impress
with peculiar God-given talents.

I knew I was but a freak of nature,
not an anointed special child
blessed with these tricky joints
by a benevolent God, a god
I don't believe in but now thank
as I contort myself on a yoga mat.

Bats

Mama thought they were bats, the black specks
that swirled in the wintertime over the smokestack
at the cotton mill beyond the railroad tracks

An eight-year-old scientist, I stood fascinated
as I watched them swoop, rise, dip, twirl, and spread,
shape shifting like faint faces in a cloud

My sisters said they would get tangled in my hair
or, worse, smell my flesh and fly my way to bite my neck,
suck my blood like a *Dark Shadows* vampire

Those mean teen sisters stayed hidden in the house,
wary of being seen wearing their transforming mud masks,
heads clutched by tightly wound brush rollers

They teased me as relentlessly as they teased
their 60s bouffant styles—the beehives and bird's nests—
taunting me with tales of little girls eaten alive

But I wasn't scared of those bats diving into my hair,
flapping and squealing with mammalian joy as they burrowed in,
better playthings than nail polish and Dippity Do

Now I know they were only common chimney swifts
returning to the smokestack to gather and roost for the night,
tucking into the warm, dropping-spattered walls

When darkness fell and the winged creatures vanished,
I crept inside to watch my sisters scrubbing away their masks,
to see again that they were just plain girls like me

REFUGE

[untitled haiku]

a mist of hairspray
women's laughter, mirrored smiles
secrets kept in style

A Prayer for a Good Day in the Beauty Shop, 1975

an abecedarian

Alma is first today—good lord, she'll want a
bun in back. That thick hair of hers is
curlier than a cucumber vine, and it'll be
dirty as a mud dauber's nest. Thank the Lord,
Estelle comes right after. Easy to please and
friendly. Always brings me something
good, like a coconut cake or socks from the
hosiery mill. Not like that stingy redhead
Irma Ruth who never tips but tells gossip
juicy as an overripe Georgia peach. She
keeps her ears open, that one. Oh Lord,
let me make it through those early
morning appointments so I can rest at
noon, eat my soup, and read *True Story*.
Olive, first to come in the afternoon, is a
prim woman with fine white hair and a
quivery voice. Lord have mercy, I try to
roll those wisps without breaking them.
Shirley's beehive will take up the most
time today. I have to tease her hair up,
up, up and shellac it with half a can of
Vita-E hairspray. I'll end the day with
Wilnita, one of my favorites. She usually
Xeroxes and brings a recipe for something
you'd never think about making yourself, like
zucchini bread. Lordy that does sound good.

In the Beauty Shop, 1963–2006

in the morning
> before the first customer of the day appeared
> and Mama opened up the shop

> the air was clear, freshened by the scent
> of cleaning the night before

throughout the day
> first one, then another, then another of Mama's ladies
> entered the shop for a cut or a color or a perm

> most were regulars who could and did tell Mama
> the stories no one else could know

> mean husbands, female troubles, money problems
> their numbing jobs at the cotton mill

> their pain rose into the air and set up there,
> trapped in the thick hairspray fog

by late afternoon
> the mist settled onto the linoleum floor,
> a sticky layer of women's words

> before closing the shop, Mama washed it away
> with Pine Sol and a string mop

All Kinds of Crazy Critters

Walking into Mama's beauty shop on a Saturday afternoon
was like visiting the zoo, Daddy said:
all kinds of crazy critters were on display out there.

He'd come back into our house hooting about the women,
settle into his recliner with a beer,
and yammer on about the customers out in the shop.

Diana Drum drooping under a hair dryer on high heat
had a face red as a baboon's butt
and a butt as broad as double-wide trailer, he said.

Florence Green was a silky hen, her golden shag hairdo
fluffed out like wings, all her features except
that squawking mouth of hers hidden by the feathers.

Patsy Crump in a skull cap with spikes of hair poking out
and slathered with pungent bleach
was a prissy porky-pine missing some spines.

Best of all was Betty Smith's massive, stinky red beehive—
she went so long between shampoos
that Daddy swore he once saw a swarm of bugs fly out.

After he stopped hee-hawing about the hairdos,
I'd take myself into my bedroom
and braid my long hair into two perfect brown pigtails.

When I sashayed past Daddy to show off my plaits,
he'd set to grunting like a fat hog in mud,
so I left him there to wallow and went to join the zoo.

Eat up with it

"She was just eat up with it,"
Mama would tell one customer about another
who died or was dying from cancer, a ravenous beast
I didn't understand when I was 10 and listening
to the prissy busybodies gossip in Mama's beauty shop.

"Eat up with it"—
I imagined African wild dogs devouring a wildebeest
from the belly in, which I knew happened because
I saw it on *Wild Kingdom*; that was being eaten, I thought,
not eat up; even then I wanted to correct words.

You could be "eat up"
with different emotions like guilt, envy, curiosity, or desire,
normal feelings that got their teeth into you and chewed,
becoming obsessions that could paralyze you,
slow your reaction time, which meant you'd be
a wild dog's dinner or its midnight snack.

We were told to "eat up"
or our food would go cold; old ladies could just eat up
cooing babies because they're so cute, grabbing at them
in their strollers, alarming young mothers; puppies, too,
and kittens—we could eat them up, turning my stomach
at the thought of calico casserole or Pekingese pâté.

"She was just eat up with it"—
the cancer that munched away at her uterus or her liver,
maybe her brain—I don't remember which,
but to speak it out loud satisfied somehow, as if to say
thank god she's the one being eaten alive, not me,
which put me in mind of the anxious wildebeest herd
watching from a careful distance as the African wild dogs,
bellies engorged, settled down in the sun to digest their prey.

Hens

On spring and autumn Saturdays
when the windows were open,
the laughter of women floated
from Mama's beauty shop,
over the breezeway,
through the screen doors,
into the house

disturbing Daddy as he read the news
or watched sports on television,
snippets of words cutting through
the hooting and carrying on—
hens cackling in a henhouse
he squawked, shaking his cockscomb,
then arising from his creaky recliner,
flapping into the kitchen to clutch
another mid-afternoon beer,
feathers rumpled, wattles in a knot

I flew away from him then
to join the women who roosted
under hair dryers or nestled
in the styling chair as Mama groomed
their fancy plumage for show—
like Silkies, Cochins, and Frizzles—
all clucking and purring and bagawking
as I perched quietly on the drink box
and listened with great attention,
learning about the ways of hens

Pixie

Sometimes they didn't notice me at all,
the women who came to Mama's beauty shop,
as I perched quietly atop the soda pop cooler
tucked into a dark nook in back, my long legs
pulled up with skinny arms around knobby
pre-teen knees, thighs close to my chest—
I thought myself a pretty fairy, resting
atop a toadstool in a mysterious dark forest,
awaiting my opportunity for mischief.

I anticipated the juicy bits a pre-teen girl
with a vivid imagination should never hear:
ailments and such with mouth-watering names
like "diverticulitis" and "hysterectomy,"
words that made my tummy twist, and stories
about husbands hammered on their jobs
at the furniture factories, about teenaged sons
caught with floozies in the shadowy recesses
of the high school, which made me tingle.

As I faced the styling chair and listened,
I filed away the women's stories for the future
without knowing why (I didn't care about them,
these women who looked ten years older
than their age, who married drunks and raised
hellions for sons and sluts for daughters),
and watched Mama until she saw my toe twitch,
locked eyes with mine, paused mid-comb-stroke,
and shushed the half-teased woman bellyaching
about her boobs and a Cross Your Heart bra.

Mama would give me her side-eyed look,
which meant I should hop off the soda pop cooler,
dust off my bottom, open the lid and take out
a Sprite without paying for it, pop off the cap
on the built-in bottle opener, take a long sip,
grab a bag of salty peanuts from the goodie jar,
flip my long hair over one shoulder, then the other,
and fly out into the sunshine and clear air.

Duchess, a German Shepherd Dog

Faithful guardian of the beauty shop,
as dignified and noble as her name,
she barked fiercely at the oil-spattered men
in the mechanics shop across the street,
men who hooted at Mama's customers
and carried on like drunk monkeys.

The beauty supply salesman would stay
in his car until Mama pulled Duchess away,
good girl with her huge paws on the window,
snout inches from the man's terror-stricken face
as she slobbered on the glass and growled
with the ferocity of a woman scorned.

She chased off more than one husband
come to fetch his wife, the customers
carrying on as they pressed rolled towels
to their dye-dripping hairlines, laughing,
wiping tears from their eyes, even that wife
who, amused, watched her man scramble.

But Duchess greeted each weary woman
with a gentle nudge and wagging tail,
bade them good-bye as they left the shop
standing straighter and freshly styled
with hair in tight buns or towering beehives
—then took her post and watched for men.

The Beauty Shop Money Box

On the day she closed the shop, she emptied me
of everything: the few bills and coins, two checks
scrawled by elderly hands. Her own hands are now slow
and liver spotted, no more with nimble, perfect fingers
that whipped hair into beehives and snipped dead ends
into a precise bob. For 46 years she opened and closed me
five days a week, trusting me with her precious money,
the precious money of cotton mill workers, schoolteachers,
and housewives who came to her home shop to feel beautiful.
Oh, happy were those days I was so stuffed with cash
she could barely latch my lid, those days of women
filling every space in the shop—the styling chair,
hulking hairdryers, love seat stacked with magazines—
women whose laughter cut through the hairspray fog,
her laughter clearest of all. I ache for her touch again,
to see her young and bustling as she juggled a perm,
two shampoo and sets, and a frosting at once; but now
she sits on a sofa in the house, an old blind cat on her lap
as she watches television, slipping into the mists of sleep
and memories. I have been retired to a dusty countertop
in the abandoned shop, my finish dull and rust splotched;
my hinges would creak if only I were opened and filled again.

Dead Air

Most of her customers talked her head off,
leaving no dead air to fill with her stories,
but this one, like very few others before,
let her prattle on and on about anything
and everything—her three smart girls,
all those kittens she needed to give away,
her mother dying too young from leukemia,
her husband, who hadn't worked all year
but brooded in front of the TV and drank.

The women needed a place to tell stories:
some were pious church ladies of course,
but most were mill workers and teachers
who had heard about her early hours and
felt safe driving the unlit country roads,
arriving at her shop at five in the morning
to have their hair washed and rolled,
dried and brushed out, teased and shaped
and shellacked for the long day ahead.

She had to stand and wait for them to leave,
had to handle their money first, had to
watch them fold dollars into their wallets
rather than give her a tip, had to listen to
them talk about their errands and chores
as they worked themselves into timeworn
cardigans, all the while wanting them to go,
anticipating the joy of the shop's air cleared
of voices before the next lady arrived.

The one today (a man!) said nary a word:
his chilly scalp yielded to her hands as she
washed his hair; his eyes—and mouth—
remained shut, he offered no judging looks,
no endless stories; he let her be, let her push
the portable dryer over his head as she sang,
chattered, laughed, sighed, complained, did
whatever she wanted to do, thankful that
the funeral home basement had no window.

DADDY

My Daddy Taught Me to Pack

1.

My daddy worked as a shipping manager, packing
train cars with odd-sized boxes of furniture.

He filled every speck of space, arranging
the cartons like shapes in a puzzle cube.

Daddy could stuff a pregnant cat into a shoe box
if need be and bury her neatly in the ground,
lined up with the other cats and kittens.

2.

Every year, we drove to the beach from the
North Carolina foothills to stay for a week
in one motel room. We used one suitcase for
the five of us: Daddy, Mama, my older sisters, me.

Swimsuits and panties were squeezed into nooks
left by Daddy's Bermuda shorts and white t-shirts,
his belts, his cartons of cigarettes, his flask.

He strapped the suitcase to the top of our gold
station wagon alongside a box perfectly packed
with plastic buckets, blow-up floats, boxes
of cereal, jars of peanut butter, white bread.

3.

The summer I was twelve and my sisters
were in college, Daddy helped me learn to pack
so light that all I took to my grandmother's house
were the clothes I wore and my flute if I could
grab it and run from him before his rage caught
me and Mama locking ourselves in the car.

I left behind the things I could make do without:
my cat and her kittens, books, clean underwear.

4.

Daddy hid his cases of beer and whiskey in the back
of the station wagon until after sundown,
sneaking them into the house during the night.

The church folk driving past and the neighbors
peering out their windows would not see.

All was packed into darkness and sealed like lips.

Too Many Kittens

she had too many too often, my cat, sometimes a handful were left,
two or three we couldn't give away, two or three that grew older

when she went into heat yet again and grew ponderous with life,
Daddy roared about stuffing kittens in a bag, tossing it in the river

when Daddy wasn't home, Mama said we could take the kittens
to the country, where they would live on a farm with kind people

we drove on bleak roads, blackberry brambles curling over ditches;
atop hills far away, small houses sat like forgotten tombstones

we stopped; Mama took my box of kittens—Cher, Barbie, Ringo—
set it by the road, ripped away the tape, ran back to me, and drove

I scrambled into the backseat, looked out the window and watched
the kittens tumble from the box, pink mouths opening and closing

they grew smaller and smaller until I couldn't see them anymore,
fading into the dusk, dissolving into the scenery like ghosts

In Deepest Sympathy

a greeting card I sent back in time to me

At this dark time
(*black cloud of hair, thunderclap in his voice, fierce wind of belt buckle meeting bone*)

no words can ease the pain
(*you're hurting her, Daddy, she's bleeding, stop, please, oh Daddy please*)

of your loss,
(*a dog not moving, fur matted with blood*)

but know that you are loved
(*he doesn't hit you, after all*)

and held in the thoughts and prayers of those who care,
(*no one helps—neighbors watch from their windows*)

those who keep you in their hearts
(*the aunts and uncles shake their heads while the church folks say it's a shame*)

and wish for you peace
(*hide the cat and her kittens*)

Different Daddies

my sisters and I had different daddies—
they were raised by a man with dreams and ambition
a young and virile man with wiry muscles
sparkly blue eyes, quick wit and ready laugh
he cooed to and cuddled his baby girls
cared for his aged father
built a beauty shop for his lovely wife
began the climb to the executive suite

I would have liked that man
would have loved having him as my daddy
been proud to speak his name at school—
he disappeared by the time my sisters were teens
when I, much younger than they, was in third grade

my daddy was a different man
a drunkard who stumbled through life
gambled away his money, lost jobs
spent months at a go doing nothing, being nothing
spat insults at his righteous mother-in-law
choked his lovely wife as I watched and pleaded
thrashed our dog with the buckle end of his belt

I wanted to like that man
wanted him to be the daddy he had been
for my sisters
the daddy I deserved

he was the daddy I got, so
he was the daddy I loved

Daddy's Little Girl

he wanted a boy but not for fishing trips or coin collecting
or whatever boys and their good daddies
did with each other in the 1970s
                                he wanted a boy to rough up

"If you were a boy, I'd take you out to that tool shed and beat you"

he said through clenched teeth many times when he was drunk
those sunny summer days when he didn't work
the year I was 12 and had nowhere to go
                                I believed he would do it
though I didn't know why I needed to be beaten
I supposed I was a convenient target
for his unfocused rage and fear
                                I knew he was afraid
that's why those mornings after he drank himself mean
I would wake him up early and tell him all about
everything he did, everything he said—
                                and he would look at me and tremble

Weeping Forsythia

When I see weeping forsythia in early spring, I see switches,
the kind I was made to choose and prepare myself,
take to Daddy for inspection.

If the stem I offered wasn't up to the task, I had to pick another—
sturdy and long enough but not too rigid at the point,
a whip-like stem.

My small hands stripped the stem bare of flowers and leaves
but left a few dangling blooms at the end,
bright and festive.

Overgrown, the bush's canes arched to the ground, created a tunnel
perfect for a small girl and her tabby cat to crawl into,
safe from his storm, held tight.

But Daddy knew my secret places, would find me, pull me out;
face molten with anger, he painted my tender legs
with bloody stripes.

After, I took the switch back to the bush aflame with yellow bells,
an offering of gratitude that it wasn't the belt
he used on the dog.

[Noise]

Your besotted shouts,
your angry bursts and fists
have exploded, pounded through
the decades since my childhood,
have kept me watchful, quiet
in too many ways

I have tiptoed,
tried not to rouse you,
listened for your raucous snores
to know I was safe as I crept
around you, past you, by you,
and through all my days

Then a board will creak,
a gust of wind rattle the screen door,
a bird crash into the picture window
—you will awaken and once more
I become a child trapped within
your intoxicated haze

A voice yelling, a face clenched,
the sound of a recliner snapping to—
they bring you back from death to me,
and for every second, every day,
I am your silent little girl
frozen in your gaze

I called you "bastard" for eight reasons

"You're a bastard" I said with a 12-year-old's spite, knowing that "bastard" like its kin "sonofabitch" was a word usually spat at men, but you wanted me to get out of the pool at the San Juan Motel in North Myrtle Beach and I didn't want to because of the following:

(1) the cute lifeguard from the beach had walked up to gaze at my golden-haired friend,

(2) I was showing off in front of that friend,

(3) you let me bring that friend even though you knew Daddy would get drunk and sunburnt and mean, which he was at that very moment,

(4) I learned the truth about you from my drunk Daddy—"conceived under a stop sign" he would throw at you after too many swigs of cheap whiskey—

(5) I didn't know what that meant until I asked you one day in the car as you drove me to get a dozen chocolate-covered, cream-filled doughnuts at the Dixie Doughnuts bakery in Whitnel,

(6) you looked over the back of the seat and told me what it meant, told me that my PaPaw hadn't really been my PaPaw because he adopted you after he married your mama,

(7) my MaMaw was a slut even though those aren't the words you used though I still thought them,

(8) I felt that everything I knew was wrong and that I wasn't who I was, and the truth hit my tummy so hard I didn't want to eat the doughnuts, which were my favorite thing ever,

so

two months later, I called you a "bastard" and you didn't get mad, just looked at me with sadness and shame while Daddy laughed, and I knew then that you could hurt too.

This is why I'm telling you about the wiener dog

it was a wiener dog turned my drunk daddy sober;
all them cats all them years couldn't do it;
mama couldn't do it no matter how hard she begged;
I couldn't do it, and I was hands-down his favorite daughter,
the one who'd get up in front of his bleary eyeballs
those mornings after a big blustery blow
when he cursed every last one of mama's relatives,
praised Richard Nixon like he was the golden calf
and threatened to drown my cat's kittens.
if his baby girl couldn't do it, I'd ask myself
when I was 12 and sitting alone as his silent audience
while my two older sisters ran off to college
and mama stayed safe in her beauty shop
next to the house where the sound of hairdryers
and women gabbing drowned out daddy's voice,
which I know blasted through the window screens,
then who on god's green earth could do it?

he was a red wiener dog I saw at the mall in Hickory,
jumping up and down in shredded newspapers,
his Dumbo hears flapping like wings as he yiped;
I pleaded and pleaded and convinced mama
to buy that wiener dog for me even though
we both knew it wasn't a good idea, even though
we both remembered what happened with
the German shepherd dog named Duchess,
but I was 13 and sad and mama thought
that little wiener dog could comfort and cheer me,
could take the place of friends and family
who would do no more than keep silent about daddy,
hoping he would one day like magic quit drinking
and they could stop looking the other way.

we took the little red wiener dog back home,
paid more money for him than I could save up
in a year from my allowance, and I held him close;
daddy still got mad, clenched his teeth, turned
as red as the wiener dog and said take it back!
but we couldn't because it was a clearance sale
on wiener dogs that day at the mall, we told him,
we couldn't return him, so daddy believed us
because he'd been drinking all day and knew nothing
about shopping of any kind whether at the mall
or the Fairway supermarket up the street,
which is where mama had to run real quick
to get puppy food while I stayed home with daddy
and clutched the little dog to my chest even though
he squirmed and whined and drew a bead on daddy,
who sat in his butt-worn leatherette recliner
making a lap the right size for a wiener puppy.

what with my sisters both run off to colleges and
leaving me to keep daddy calm all by myself,
I figured I would have to take the wiener dog
to school and band practice and church with me
so daddy wouldn't do harm to him even though
he wasn't a kitten and we gave him the name
daddy picked, which was Theodore Rustivon,
and we called him Teddy and registered him proper
with the AKC even though it didn't really mean much
but sounded good along with his fancy name:
this is our dog Theodore Rustivon, who is called Teddy
and who is registered proper with the AKC so there.

but it turned out that daddy fell in love with the dog,
teaching him to play a game called putt putt,
which involved Teddy laying sideways under a chair
with his paws sticking out from under the dust flap
and daddy rolling a tiny rubber ball to him,
which Teddy would either (a) catch in his mouth
then flick back out with a paw or (b) bat back out
if it came in under his chin and he couldn't catch it;
either way he never missed and that tickled daddy
who loved to watch golf and play real putt putt
at the miniature golf course up in Lenoir
where he often took me and mama and laughed
when my pink ball got stuck in the windmill blades.

mama didn't feature leaving Teddy with daddy
so she kept him in the beauty shop with her
and set up a Ritz-Carlton for wiener dogs there
to keep him happy and to allow all the customers
to make cootchy-coo noises at him as if he were a baby
instead of a dog who knew he could get away
with peeing and pooping all over the shag carpets
in my bedroom, which was in our house next door,
and chewing up Kleenex and Tampax from the trash
(daddy never quite got over finding chewed-up remains
one Sunday after church and I learned a new trick
for making daddy go hide in the bedroom with his bottle
rather than sit in his recliner and go to get a nip
from the bedroom closet in between bouts of telling me
why he wished I had been a boy named Wesley Kent
instead of a girl so he could beat the crap out of me).

one day it got to be that daddy couldn't bear
to be parted from Teddy and he got twitchy
when mama kept the dog in the shop all day
so that daddy couldn't play putt putt with him
or hold him on his lap when he thought nobody
was looking, which of course I always was doing
because I was a true blue teenager and
it was my job to be snoopy and see things
I wasn't supposed to see like the church ladies
out in the shop reading *True Story* magazine
while they sat under the big hulking hairdryers
with their legs crossed real tight and their mouths
making an "o" shape and eyes big as eggs.

daddy would go out to the shop pretending
to check on mama but really wanting to pet Teddy,
who was usually curled up on a customer's lap,
which was a place daddy couldn't pet
without consequences which involved mama
chasing him out with a rattail comb held like a knife,
and daddy would grab Teddy and run into the house
where he settled into his recliner, petted the dog,
watched golf on TV and before he knew it
he hadn't taken a drink of Scotch whiskey all day.

those big round brown puppy dog eyeballs
and floppy little ears were miracle workers.

so anyway, you asked about that picture portrait
of me in a fancy church dress, sitting on the floor,
legs tucked sideways under the big loose skirt,
which mama draped all around me in a circle
like icing on a doll cake as I cradled the wiener dog
very gracefully, if I might say so myself, in my arms
with my nails freshly painted the color Lauren Hutton
wore in *Vogue* magazine the month before
—you asked me why I was holding a little dog
in my picture portrait the year I turned 17
when both my sisters were with their new husbands
and mama was with daddy in their portraits and we're all smiling
and daddy hadn't had a drink of whiskey in two years and
Theodore Rustivon got to be in his own picture portrait
all by himself lit just so to make his eyes look bigger
and I didn't get a solo picture, but it doesn't matter
because, as I said out loud to you just a minute ago,
daddy hadn't had a drink of whiskey in two years.

MAMA, AFTER DADDY

To the elderly hairdresser

you stood each day, drawing delight
from the tired souls of women who toiled
in cotton mills and furniture factories

you stood late into the evening,
teasing hair with tired hands, stooping
over the sink, rinsing away worries as you
gazed into your house just across the breezeway

you stood as you trimmed ends
or touched up roots, offering solace
while your customers made excuses
for bruises and busted lips, leaving no room
for proud stories about your three girls

you stood so long your veins weakened,
taking you off your legs and away
from the shop while you lay in bed
and healed the ulcers that plague you still
in your eighties, making you fret about
losing the customers styled by other hands

you stood for five decades, coaxing life
from limp locks, teasing brittle strands
into beehive glory, greeting the first lady
before dawn, saying good-bye to the last
after dark, squeezing housework into the spaces
between permanents, watching for your youngest
to come home from school, bursting with gossip

you sit now, after all those years of aching
to get off your feet, to retire, to rest—you sit
because you cannot stand, your dowager's hump
and poor balance dropping you to the floor,
leaving you to be swept away like shorn curls,
forgotten as the endless TV shows you watch
or the romance novels you fall asleep over
while you sit, sit, sit and wish that you could stand

Obituary: Mickey's Beauty Salon, Hudson, NC, 1963–2012

How did we think Mickey's shop would die?
did we think she would go beautifully, softly, quietly—
fading into the sunset like temporary dye on gray hair?
Did we all think Mickey would host a picnic potluck,
inviting every single one of us from her almost 50 years
of washing and trimming, rolling up and drying,
dyeing and permanent rodding until our scalps screamed?
What were we expecting—a parade in the shop's honor,
with the high school band blaring and majorettes twirling,
with floats bearing beauties and groups hoisting banners,
all wending their way from the First Baptist Church to the shop,
stopping at her door and cheering when the mayor
read a proclamation and handed her a key to the town?

How were we to know that she would suffer
the most disgusting of indignities, with a sulfurous stench
and sprays of excrement festooning her aging walls?
Could we have predicted that a good-for-nothing scofflaw
with a septic-tank-sucking truck and three beers in his belly
would pump the uphill neighbor's load into a manhole
and push the sludge on down to Mickey's house and shop,
where it burped from toilets and sinks and sent Mickey—
a widow living alone—into her yard yodeling for help?
Who on god's green earth would imagine that familiar linoleum
buried under a foot of stinking brown sewage?

Now we are left to remember Mickey's Beauty Salon,
just us—the women who sat still and tall in the styling chair
for beehives in the 60s, Farah Fawcett shags in the 70s,
and the Aqua-Net bangs and big hair from the 80s that we dread
to come across in family photos and high school yearbooks—
as our skin becomes polka dotted and thin as chiffon,

as we think back on the ruckus of three or more women
competing for Mickey's attention amidst the roar of hairdryers,
as we pen this obituary without knowing how to find words
to do them right, both Mickey and the shop, without knowing
how to say more than you deserved a more dignified end.
Rest in peace, our good friend.

After I slept in Mama and Daddy's bed

Mama told me to put my suitcase in their room,
      the one she and Daddy slept in for more than 60 years—

she had been sleeping in the room that was mine,
she would tell me the reason tomorrow.

So I slept in their room, in their bed.

Mama told me she woke up in the middle of the night,
      felt Daddy next to her though he'd been dead seven years,

he was talking to her, his mouth was silent but moving,
he leaned over her, his eyes blacked out in the dark.

She told me all of that after I slept so well in their bed.

Mama told me that seeing Daddy didn't scare her,
      but made her dread bedtime and caused strange dreams,

he showed up again and again, every few nights,
he kept at her all through the night, kept her awake for hours.

She told me all of that after I slept so well in their bed.

Mama told me when she woke up the last night in that bed,
      she felt him walking across her feet, up her legs—

she told me all that had happened in that room,
she told me she should forgive him and forget but couldn't.

After she told me all of that, after I had slept so well in their bed,
      I slept in their room and in their bed again, and I felt
      everything.

I hear her voice calling

I hear my mother's voice calling
all 85 years of love, ache, and worry
calling into the vacant, lonely air
Blackie Blackie Blackie
getting no response, no soft padding of paws
through bone dry leaves, no barely heard
feline trill of *here I come*
I hear your voice calling

when she tells me over two hundred miles
of telephone line that a neighbor
waited all day to call about seeing Blackie
laying in that ditch out there this morning
hit by a car whose driver didn't slow
for a cat on his morning rounds
I hear her voice calling

when she tells me about phoning town hall
asking the man who answered
what did they do with my Blackie
what do they do with the animals by the road
and I know she couldn't say the word *dead*
I hear her voice calling

when she says she told the man
I want to bury him here at home
in the back yard with my other cats
I think *no no no no no* and wait
for her to weep as she tells me
the awful truth, that dead cats are thrown
in the dump with all the other trash
I hear her voice calling

when she doesn't weep, only tells me
in the saddest, softest mother's voice
he said they have places out in the country
where they bury animals, nice places
but he didn't know where Blackie got buried
I think what a mercy from a stranger
whose job is to speak plain about dead cats
that even over the telephone
he heard my mother's voice calling

Please don't cut down the cedar tree

a hastily scribbled note left at the front door

To the buyer of my parents' house:

You've bought ghosts—
my mother's, my father's, my two sisters', mine,
as well as the spirits of two dogs, two white mice,
two parakeets, and at least fifty cats and kittens.
We'll live with you always in this house,
on the back porch, in the camel cricket-infested crawl space,
in Mama's sewage-flooded then gutted beauty shop
(don't ask—you don't want to know).

We'll float through the bedroom
where daddy kept his whiskey hidden in the closet,
which had a door that creaked every time
he opened it, squealed like a kitten
being thrown against the old wooden toolshed.
I hope someone oiled those hinges for you
so you don't have to hide under the bed when you hear
that door opening and closing and opening and closing.

You've bought the painful secrets told in the beauty shop;
the cartwheels clumsily turned in the back yard;
the German shepherd dog given away
because she chased cars and hated all men;
the breeze that blew across my bedroom,
in through one screened window and out the other;
the lightning bugs blinking and dying in a jar by my bed
as I lay frozen, listening to Daddy's rage.

You've also bought a thousand women's voices,
their laughter that floated from the beauty shop
into my bedroom in the summer, the love
and purpose they gave my mother.
You've bought the pet cemetery in the back yard,
where beloved cats and a wiener dog lie buried
near granite markers and a crumbling concrete angel.
You've bought the walnut and pecan trees,
the half-acre garden that hasn't been planted for years.
Maybe you will plant corn, tomatoes, and cucumbers there?

And the cedar tree in the front yard—
the tallest, strongest, most-loved cedar tree in the world.
My sisters played apartments in its limbs sixty years ago,
its span and depth so great they could live there
for an afternoon, make their plans to grow up and leave.
I came too late for apartment living, but I climbed
and climbed and climbed that cedar tree
until I reached the sky, until I knew I was safe.

Wash her hair

a pandemic plea

For god's sake, don't you know? She was a hairdresser!
Hair was her life, doing hair gave her life, doing hair was her joy;
her own hair was always clean and perfectly styled,
a model of her skill with scissors and comb, with rollers and spray.

Now you let her sit—behind the smudged window
of this care facility, this place of care, this place that should care
about everything that makes her healthy and happy,
everything that makes her heart beat—out of our reach,
where we (her daughters) can't touch her, can't wash her hair,
trim the ends, blow it dry, and curl it with an iron.

We can only stand outside in thick heat that wilts
our own careful hairdos, press our hands against the glass,
mouth the words to her because she can't hear us
      —it's ok mama, it's ok, we haven't left you, we're still here.

She's slumped in a wheelchair, her hair a mess of dirty oily wisps,
her eyes downcast, hands trembling in her lap, head shaking
              —she knows! she knows how she looks!

You removed the mask and abandoned her there
so her breath wouldn't touch you; now her lips are moving,
and we can't understand, can't hear her through the glass,
can't know for sure but can only guess that she wants someone,
anyone, to make her feel alive and whole again,
to caress her scalp, to hear her stories—to wash her hair.

By flowers

a reverse abecedarian

zinnias, Mama says, are her favorite flowers;

yesterday her most beloved was
Xerochrysum, the paper daisy or strawflower,
which Mama knew the scientific name for because her aunt,
Verlee, was an amateur horticulturist,
unusually expert at pinching leaves and stems
to root in her greenhouse—
                                    and suddenly Mama most prefers
Scabiosa, or pincushion flower, but no—*Salvia,* she says,
red spikes, vibrant and thrilling, as she recalls rare
quiet moments in Verlee's many gardens, among
peonies and tulips in the spring border, while her other aunt,
Orene, sat in the shade sipping sweet iced tea,
nodding as Mama headed to the vegetable garden to set out
marigolds between the rows of tomato seedlings;

late in the day, the listing of flowers falls away, light fades,
keening begins, sundowning that closes the morning glory's bloom,
jabbering nonsense that blossoms into rage—
                                        help her remember
iris, purple bearded lovelies she planted behind her beauty shop,
hope she will recall how they rebloomed as perfect as before,
give her the courage to—

forget-me-not! she is back if only briefly,
eager to remind me that the most special flowers,
daylilies, are for daughters or maybe mothers, she isn't sure,
calls up one more favorite—
                                    then by flowers, our therapy is done
because she has remembered from zinnia, a symbol of enduring, to
anemone, fragile flower of such short life

Mama's Baby

she was your baby girl
a precious gift from the gods
who knew where to drop cats and kittens
unloved and starving for care
right away you took her in and loved her
the wee mewling fluff of black fur
loved her years later when she was old like you
tended to her when she became deaf and blind
fretted when she ate and when she didn't
woke her when she slept so soundly
(Baby! Baby! Wake up! Baby!)
wept when you were taken from her
yourself to be watched and nursed
like a baby

your Baby came to me then
hundreds of miles away from you
folded into my own house of cats
gifted at one time or another from the gods
I came to love her as she bravely explored
as she bumped into this and that
meeting each male cat and hissing at his smell
finding her spot in bed with me at night
waking me with tufted taps and soft trills
and then that morning just after three
(You! You! Wake up! You!)
making sure I knew you were leaving
after stopping first to say good-bye
to your babies

LEGACY

Armored

for Kent Craig

thank you, daddy, for my heart,
a diabolical ironclad beetle beating itself
against my chest, bearing 39,000 times its weight
in dread

if I were an ironclad beetle,
I could endure 5,304,000 pounds on my bones,
suffer the world's shattering blows—
but I am fragile flesh

not an interlocked jigsaw puzzle
like the ironclad's outer skeleton, though my heart
has pieced itself together, welded the cracks of countless breaks,
become uncrushable

Well-Bred

Thanks to my daddy
I'm a bitch never bred,
wide in the hips
like him and fertile—
but he ruined me
for children, drank away
my brood, drowned
my progeny in whiskey,
sired doubt and fear
about their bloodline,
chilled my heat
when I was in season
and open to the rut,
stifled my fecundity
so he could scratch
his thirsty itch.

My Feral Children

my father silenced my voice, stilled my tongue
chained my words with his rage, made me hide myself away
a silent girl, a mute ghost floating through childhood
then decade after decade after decade
soundlessly starving—until the poems

for 56 years, the poems were locked away
like feral children hidden in basements, sheds, bedrooms
with windows covered over by cardboard or plywood
children kept in darkness and fed stale bread or rotting fruit
just enough to keep them alive and hoping
reaching for light, waiting for air
longing to be embraced and nurtured
dreaming of having a voice, of hearing their own voices
of knowing the wonder and nourishment of sound
dicing words, crisping consonants
or pulling and stretching vowels like dough
rolling syntax around in their mouths
like succulent candies

I didn't know they were there

the words came years after my father died
from a bad heart, no figure of speech that—
the verses emerged sizzling and steaming
spiced by sibilance, fragrant with fricatives
savory syllable stews of flavorful phonemes

satiated, no longer ravenous, my feral children are free
I relish their rhythms, savor their rhymes, watch them grow
then leave me

That First Poem

I remember—but lost to the decades since—
the first poem I wrote, in 1968, the poem
that made my daddy so proud, the poem
about how Richard Nixon would save us all
from air smog. I wrote that dear little poem,
with flowers and butterflies drawn alongside
and happy stick figures too, on light purple
lined paper, and I was so happy when daddy
smiled and nodded his head, though later on
I disappointed him when I became a Democrat,
which to him held no value at all, much like poetry.
After he died, when I could do things
that would have made him frown, when I
no longer cared what he thought even though
for decades I had been an adult, an adult
who *still* wanted to make her daddy smile,
I became a poet.

My Mama Taught Me to Smile

notes for a brief slide deck depicting scenes of Mama smiling

1. At 6 a.m. she greets this woman with a smile. Mama is happy to see this customer enter her beauty shop. Notice the woman's greasy hair, likely unwashed since her last visit two weeks ago. Imagine the stench.

2. Notice the clock on the wall—8:37 p.m. The window behind Mama is dark, as it was when she entered the shop that morning. Her hands hover high above this woman's head as she teases the beehive. Imagine the strain on her shoulders, the ache in her back, the numbness of her feet. Mama's smile lights the darkness.

3. She carries a heap of dirty towels and her money box heavy with coins into the house, past Daddy snoring in his recliner and a young teen (me) watching television. Mama glances sideways at the girl, her smile a ray of love.

4. Yes, yes, I know—a man in the shop! Mama is washing Daddy's hair on Saturday afternoon, a weekly ritual. With his head back in the sink and mama bent over him, his hands locked over his belly, legs spread wide, he looks harmless. He has said something funny, which he could do, and Mama smiles down at him. Already the floral smell of whiskey is on his breath.

5. Daddy has dragged her out of the beauty shop, used his fists on her there under the old pear tree. Two customers run toward them, one with plastic cape flapping and permanent rods dangling, as Mama, lip bleeding, looks up at him with pleading eyes and a smile so heartbreaking . . .

6. Her head is blurry because she is shaking it, but the smile is clearly there. See the flash of beautiful white teeth? A teenager (me again) clutches her arm and appears to be wailing. Mama is saying *I can't leave my shop, I can't leave my shop, I can't leave my shop.*

7.–18. No notes for these slides.

19. Mama and Daddy's 60th anniversary photo, taken at the First Baptist Church. Daddy hadn't had a drink in more than twenty years. They stand close, do as they are told, and "smile!" at the camera. [Aside: Daddy died less than a year later.]

20. The back of my head blocks Mama's face. You shouldn't see her face—the mortician did a horrible job, stretching her lips into a grimace. On the other side of that long gray hair, I look down at her, and I smile, as she taught me to do.

Every Other Sunday at 4

When the phone rang every other Sunday at 4,
my college suitemates let me answer. My parents were calling.
For 20 minutes we talked, no more than 20 minutes;
that's all the time Daddy allowed for me. Long distance calls
were expensive in the '70s. "Hey, sugar!" Mama's smile so clear
in her voice but then "Here's your Daddy." She handed me to him
for two minutes of awkward talk about grades and money.
In minute three, he gave me back to Mama, her words frantic
as she eyed the clock and crammed two weeks' of family news
and beauty shop stories into 16 minutes. Then Daddy's voice
commanding—*Time to hang up! Go on now!*—and
Mama pleading to talk to her baby just a little longer.
She always needed that entire last minute to say good-bye, as she
clutched the receiver, held me close. If she called during the week,
I knew a relative had died or a customer had cancer or
some other horrible thing had happened. We did this for decades
after I graduated, as I stayed away from my hometown.
When they were old, I was the one who made the call.
Now, with both parents gone and no children of my own,
every other Sunday at 4, I still wait for the phone to ring.

THE PRAYER

On Trying to Write a Prayer for Forgiving My Parents

an abecedarian

Ancestors, I'm told, are
blameless, shouldn't be
condemned for the harm we
do ourselves—our
estrangement from love, our
faithless souls that send
godliness packing, our inability to
heal our inherited wounds.
I'm told to pray, to begin my
journey toward self-redemption.
Karma tells me otherwise: my
lineage is damned, my
maternal and paternal genes
nested together, beget
ornate and tightly stitched
patterns of pieced troubles, a
quilted bedcover to lie under,
resplendent with generational
shame and sordid adornments.
Try as I might, I cannot
understand whatever scant
virtue comes from the absolving.
What do I forgive when
X ticks all the parental boxes?
You, God, shouldn't ravage my
zen—this prayer is all about me.

About the Author

Born and raised in Caldwell County, North Carolina, Daun Daemon is the youngest of three sisters who came of age in their Mama's beauty shop, a one-chair operation attached to their house by a breezeway. When her Mama wasn't looking, she would eavesdrop on the women and sneak a pack of nabs from the shop's snack jar and a bottle of Sun Drop from the drink box. Those days in the beauty shop stayed with her for decades, inspiring much of her poetry and fiction.

Daemon has published short stories in *Flock, Dead Mule School, Literally Stories,* and *Delmarva Review* among others. Her poems have appeared in *Third Wednesday, Typehouse Literary Review, Remington Review, Deep South Magazine, Into the Void, Peeking Cat Literary, Amsterdam Quarterly, Adanna,* and numerous other journals and anthologies. She teaches scientific communication at North Carolina State University, where she was a past director of the Young Writers Workshop and founder of the Teen Writers Workshop. Daemon lives in Raleigh with her husband and, at the time of this writing, three cats.

www.ingramcontent.com/pod-product-compliance
Lightning Source LLC
Chambersburg PA
CBHW030910170426
43193CB00009BA/803